FRIENDS
OF ACPL

Nature's Children

SCORPIONS

Amanda Harman

GROLIER
EDUCATIONAL

FACTS IN BRIEF

Classification of Scorpions

Class:	*Arachnid* (scorpions, spiders, and their relations)
Order:	*Scorpiones* (scorpions)
Family:	There are eight families of scorpions.
Genus:	There are many genera of scorpions.
Species:	There are more than 1,300 species of scorpions.

World distribution.   Scorpions can be found worldwide, but especially in the tropics and subtropics.

Habitat.   Mainly deserts, forests, and grasslands, hidden under rocks or the bark of dead trees, or in caves.

Distinctive physical characteristics.   Large arachnids with a long body divided into segments. A pair of big, clawlike pincers at the front and a stinging tail often held forward over the back. Body color is usually brown or black.

Habits.   Scorpions are nocturnal and generally solitary.

Diet.   Spiders, other scorpions, and large insects, such as crickets and cockroaches. Some hunt small lizards and mice.

© 2001 Brown Partworks Limited
Printed and bound in U.S.A.
Edited by Jens Thomas

Published by:

GROLIER
EDUCATIONAL

Sherman Turnpike, Danbury, Connecticut 06816

Library of Congress Cataloging-in-Publication Data

Scorpions.
    p. cm. -- (Nature's children. Set 7)
  ISBN 0-7172-5547-6 (alk. paper) -- ISBN 0-7172-5531-X (set)
  1. Scorpions--Juvenile literature. [1. Scorpions.] I. Grolier Educational (Firm) II. Series.

QL458.7 S36 2001
595.4'6--dc21

00-067246

Contents

Few small animals are as feared and hated as the scorpion. Many people think of scorpions as evil and vicious creatures with a terrifying sting that can kill a person. It is very unfair to think of scorpions like this, though. Most scorpion stings will only kill large insects—the favorite food of scorpions—and are not strong enough to seriously hurt humans. Scorpions are also very shy animals that prefer to keep away from people whenever possible. They will lash out with their stinging tail only if they feel that they are in danger.

Not everyone hates scorpions, and some people even like to keep them as pets. The most popular type to keep as a pet is the imperial scorpion. It is one of the largest scorpions in the world! Keep reading this book, and you will find out the true facts about this fascinating animal.

Opposite page: A scorpion's stinging tail and powerful claws make the animal look very fierce.

Giant Ancestors

Opposite page:
Scorpions have been on Earth for around four times longer than their spider relatives. The spiders we see today have only existed on the planet for around 70 million years.

Scorpions are extremely ancient creatures, and their close relatives have been on Earth for a very long time. Over 400 million years ago their cousins the sea scorpions were roaming through the oceans. Sea scorpions were huge animals that sometimes grew as long as six and a half feet (2 meters). They were fierce hunters that caught and fed on smaller creatures that lived in the oceans. The last of the sea scorpions died out many millions of years ago, but around 300 million years ago the direct ancestors of today's scorpions first appeared. These early land scorpions probably looked much like the ones we see today.

Scorpions belong to a group of animals called the arachnids. Spiders, mites, ticks, and daddy-longlegs all belong to this group of animals as well. Many people wrongly think that scorpions and spiders are insects. They are not insects, but they are closely related to them—arachnids and insects belong to a much larger group of animals called the arthropods.

Where Scorpions Live

There are more than 1,300 different species (types) of modern-day scorpions. They are found in nearly all parts of the world. Scorpions can survive deep under the snow in areas up to 16,000 feet (5,000 meters) high in mountains such as the Andes. However, scorpions love warmth, and most species live in tropical forests, grasslands, and deserts. In North America there are around 90 different species of scorpion. They are found across the United States and up into southern parts of Canada. The main places in the world that scorpions don't live are the Arctic in the Northern Hemisphere and New Zealand and Antarctica in the Southern Hemisphere.

Opposite page: *A thick-tailed scorpion wanders through the Kalahari Desert in Africa.*

Hiding Away

This black scorpion from southern Europe has found a crack in the rock just big enough to hide in.

Scorpions tend to hide away most of the time in caves or in cracks and crevices under rocks, logs, or the bark of dead trees. Desert species in the American Southwest have strong, broad feet covered with comblike hairs. They use them for digging burrows in the sand and gravel of the desert. These scorpions spend most of their time in underground burrows. Being underground protects them from very high or very low temperatures, which would otherwise kill them. Other scorpions are able to climb trees, while some species enter people's houses and live in their bedding, shoes, and clothes!

Although all scorpions are land animals, some are often found down on the rocky sea shore. They live under stones and among the plants that grow along the coast. Some of these scorpions are even able to survive if they are covered by the tide for short periods of time.

Nighttime Is the Right Time

Scorpions do not have a bony skeleton inside their body like we do. Instead, they are held together by a hard outer shell known as an exoskeleton. Although the exoskeleton is extremely tough, it is also very light and flexible so that the scorpion can move around.

Scorpions are nocturnal, which means that they are active at night. During the day they spend their time resting in their hideouts. These animals generally live on their own. Most species are not particularly sociable, and the only groups of scorpions you are likely to see are mothers with their offspring. Whenever two scorpions come face to face, they will often fight aggressively with each other until one of them is dead. A few species, however, may burrow together or gather in groups through the winter.

Opposite page:
A yellow desert scorpion. The movable joints between the different sections of a scorpion's body allow them to get around surprisingly quickly.

Biggest and Smallest

Some scorpions are the largest of the arachnids. Although the smallest species—*Microbuthus pusillus* from the Middle East—reaches just half an inch (1.3 centimeters) in length, most other species are much bigger than this. The largest scorpions are probably the imperial scorpion, which lives in Africa and reaches over 2 ounces (57 grams) in weight, and the rock scorpion, which comes from South Africa and grows longer than 8 inches (20 centimeters). This is nothing compared to the earliest land-dwelling scorpions, some of which were 16 inches (40 centimeters) long. That is about the length of a large rabbit!

Adult male and female scorpions look very similar to each other. However, you can tell them apart, because the female is usually larger and has a shorter tail than the male.

Bits and Pieces

Insects have a body made of three main parts. They are the head, a middle section with legs called the thorax, and a big end section called the abdomen. The scorpion has a body that is only divided into two main parts. That is because in the group of animals called the arachnids the head and the thorax are joined together to form a single big section called the cephalothorax.

The cephalothorax carries the mouthparts, several pairs of eyes, the claws, and four pairs of legs. It also has a pair of comblike structures called the pectines attached to its underside. Unlike that of spiders and mites, however, the scorpion's abdomen is very long and divided into 12 sections, or segments.

Opposite page:
A forest scorpion from Australia.
It is easy to see the different sections that make up a scorpion's body.

A Sting in the Tail

Opposite page:
*The sting of a giant
hairy scorpion
from America.*

Perhaps the scorpion's most famous
characteristic is its tail. It is long and slender,
and made up of several segments, ending in a
rounded, stinging spine. The sharp spine is
hollow and works a little like the injection
needles that are used to give shots in the
hospital. In most scorpions poison, or venom,
is stored in a large sac under the spine. When a
scorpion stings its victim, the spine sticks into
the skin, and muscles pump the venom in
through the wound.

An imperial scorpion. A scorpion has very powerful muscles in its claws so that it can crush insects and other animals it likes to eat.

Dangerous Claws

The two legs right at the front of a scorpion are not used for walking at all. Instead, they have grown into a pair of large, dangerous-looking claws, or pincers. They are probably the second of the scorpion's most recognizable features. They are used for grabbing hold of things, such as an insect when hunting or another scorpion during mating. The other four pairs of legs are for walking, and each one has a small claw at the end of the foot. These claws help the scorpion get a grip on the ground when it is moving around.

Scorpions are usually colored to blend in with the soil, sand, or wood of their surroundings. Because of this most scorpions are colored black or a shade of brown. Those in desert areas are often yellowish.

Lobster Look-alike

The body of the scorpion is long and flattened. That means it is perfectly designed for crawling into the small crevices where the scorpion likes to hide.

The scorpion's body looks a little like that of a lobster or crayfish. However, there are several ways that you can tell the difference between these animals. The main giveaway is that scorpions are found on land, while lobsters and crayfish always live in water. As well as this, if you look closely, you will see that lobsters and crayfish have long feelers, or antennae, on their head, while scorpions do not. Scorpions also usually hold their long, segmented tail forward over their back. The tails of lobsters and crayfish are fan-shaped and stick out straight behind.

Glowing in the Dark

No one knows why, but all adult scorpions glow in the dark if you shine ultraviolet (UV) light on them. This is very handy for scientists when they are trying to find scorpions to study. They just shine a special UV flashlight in the darkness and look out for the brightly glowing scorpions!

Unlike many animals that are active at night, scorpions do not have good eyesight to help them see well in the dark. Most scorpions have two eyes on top of their head and up to five pairs of "simple" eyes arranged along the side of their head. Even with all these eyes a scorpion's eyesight is probably only good enough to tell the difference between daytime and nighttime. Some scorpions live in caves all their lives and are completely blind.

Opposite page: *Because their eyes are so simple, scorpions cannot see the details of their surroundings.*

Seeing by Touch

Instead of sight, the best sense that a scorpion has is touch. There are special touch sensors on the animal's mouthparts, while tiny hairs all over the body detect movements in the surrounding air. These hairs, which are mainly on the claws and tail, are particularly thick and bristly in the so-called hairy scorpions of the southwestern United States.

Even more important than these sensitive hairs, however, are the detectors on the scorpion's feet and the pectines. The pectines look a little like two combs that are attached to the underside of the scorpion's body. Together, the detectors on the scorpion's feet and the pectines allow the scorpion to pick up any ground vibrations caused by the approach of prey (animals the scorpion likes to eat) or enemies.

This is a hairy scorpion from Arizona. Some people think that a scorpion's pectines are so sensitive that they can even detect moisture in the air.

Good Vibrations

Scorpions are complete carnivores, which means that they eat only the living body tissues of other animals. They can pick up vibrations in the ground so well that they can use them in hunting. When a victim is moving around nearby, it makes the ground vibrate, or shake. The vibrations travel to the scorpion's pectines and feet detectors, but they arrive at different times. This tiny time difference allows the scorpion to pinpoint exactly where its prey is. The scorpion then moves in slowly for the kill.

When a scorpion gets within striking range of its prey, it lunges forward and grabs it with its large claws. If the victim is a fairly big animal, the scorpion will use the sting in its tail to attack it before tearing it to pieces and crushing the flesh with its jaws!

Opposite page: *This imperial scorpion has caught a snake for its dinner.*

Making a Meal of It

As the scorpion crushes the body tissues of its prey, it produces a digestive fluid. The fluid is used to break down the food into liquid so that the scorpion can suck it up easily with its mouthparts. When it has finished eating, the scorpion leaves behind a ball of hard material that it cannot eat. Eating just this one meal can take as long as half a night. Once the scorpion has fed, it will not need to hunt again for several months. Some scorpions may not need to eat again for an entire year!

Although they are crafty hunters, scorpions cannot run after their prey if it escapes. Scorpions hunt mainly spiders, centipedes and millipedes, and insects such as crickets, cockroaches, moths, flies, and beetles. Some of the larger scorpions, such as the giant desert hairy scorpion, will attack bigger creatures. They will make a meal of mice, lizards, and snakes whenever they can. Some species even feed on other scorpions.

Buzz Off!

Although scorpions use their stinging tail mainly on creatures they have caught to eat, they sometimes need to use it to defend themselves from other hunters. Raiding army ants, large spiders, praying mantises, frogs, salamanders, lizards, snakes, shrews, bats, and birds such as owls all like to make a meal of a scorpion whenever they get the chance. Some scorpion species use clicking and buzzing noises to warn other animals that they are armed with a nasty sting.

Those scorpion species with particularly strong venom in their sting can affect even animals much larger than themselves, such as monkeys and humans. Some animals that hunt scorpions have learned how to pull off the stinging tail before they eat the scorpion.

Deadly Poison

There are two types of venom in scorpion stings. The most dangerous of them works by acting on its victim's nervous system. It is known as a neurotoxin. If you were stung with this kind of venom, it would gradually travel around your body in your bloodstream, and you would feel sick and sweaty and begin to drool. The area around the sting would be extremely painful at first, and then it would begin to feel numb. The muscles in your throat would feel as though they were getting tighter and tighter, and eventually your skin would turn blue. All this might be stopped by taking a medicine called an antivenin. If you were unlucky enough to be in a place where there was no antivenin, your heart would give out, and you might die.

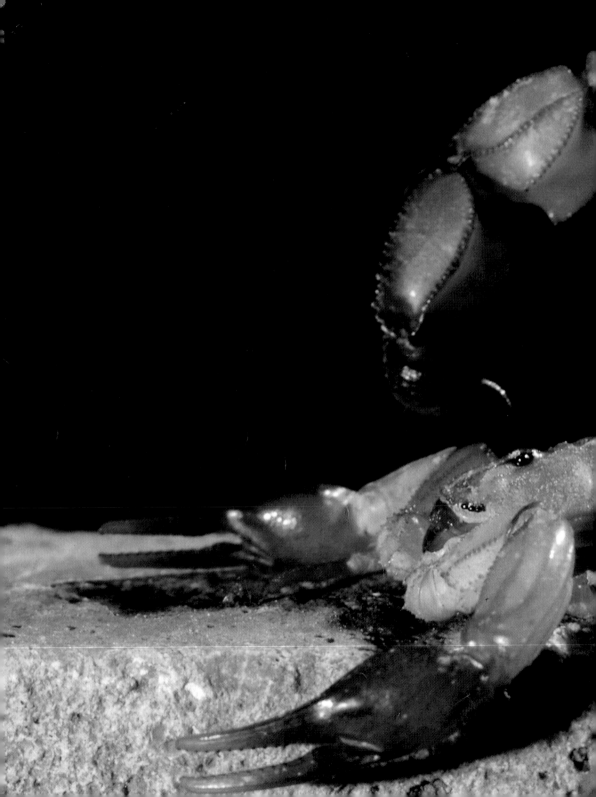

Stinging Humans

Opposite page:
Watch out!
In countries where
there are lots of
scorpions, you
need to be careful
if you walk around
with bare feet.

Although many people are frightened of scorpions because of their venom, these animals attack humans only if they are suddenly disturbed or feel threatened.

The stings of most scorpions are deadly only for insects, anyway, and very few species are dangerous to humans. The main scorpions to be wary of are the Durango scorpion, which is found in Mexico, and the bark scorpion from Arizona, New Mexico, and Mexico. They are the most deadly of any stinging animals in this area of the United States, and several people have died as a result of being stung by them. The Sahara scorpion of Africa is also an extremely dangerous species: its venom can kill a person in just a few hours.

A bark scorpion from the Arizona Desert in North America. It is sometimes called the "Arizona deadly scorpion."

Harmless Stings

Stings from most scorpion species are no worse than those of bees or wasps and can be treated with the same medicines. The pain, tingling, and swelling caused by the scorpion sting can also be relieved by covering the area with icy water. The symptoms will normally disappear completely within 24 hours. Some people are allergic to the stings of insects and scorpions. They can die even if they are stung by a normally quite harmless scorpion.

Most scorpions do not seem to be affected by their own venom if they accidentally sting themselves. In some species the male may stroke his partner with his tail during mating. He may even sting her as part of his courtship.

Tango for Two

Opposite page: *Once they have finished mating, male and female scorpions go their separate ways. The female will have to give birth and raise the babies alone.*

In many species a male and female scorpion perform a kind of "dance" before mating. This dance lasts for a long time—sometimes for several days! With their outstretched claws locked together, they move backward and forward over the ground, sometimes with their dangerous tails entwined. Although this looks very romantic, it is mainly so that the male can avoid being stung—or even eaten—by his partner! The movement also sweeps the ground clear so that the male can pass his sperm easily to the female. He drops it on the ground in a large packet called a spermatophore and then pulls the female forward over it so that she can take the package up into her body. Once this strange mating ritual has finished, the male leaves as quickly as he can. If he is not quick enough in leaving, the female may eat him!

Piggyback

After mating, the fertilized eggs begin to develop inside the female's body. While they are developing, they receive food directly from their mother's stomach. Up to a year and a half later the baby scorpions are born live, using their stings to force their way out of the skin covering them. In some species the female gives birth to just a few offspring at a time, while in others as many as a hundred are born over a few days. Their mother immediately rests on the ground so that her babies can climb up her claws and onto her back.

Like spiders, female scorpions make excellent parents. The youngsters remain on their mother's back for around two weeks, being carried everywhere. They are not fed by her, however. During this time they use up food reserves in their own body. At this stage they are very soft and whitish, and would make a tasty meal for many animals, so their mother has to protect them fiercely.

Opposite page:
A scorpion mother carries her young on her back.

Growing Up

Opposite page:
As they get older, baby scorpions lose the bright, white color they have when they are first born.

By the time two weeks are up, the youngsters will have grown much larger and shed their hard outer skeleton. This process is called molting. A new tough covering will grow in place of the old one, but this one will have a little more room so that they can grow even bigger. The young scorpions are now old enough to care for themselves, and they clamber down from their mother's back, and all go their separate ways in search of food.

In some species the young scorpions will be ready to mate and have their own offspring within about seven months. During this time they will have molted their old skin and grown a new one as many as seven or eight times. In other species it takes up to four years before the youngsters become fully adult. In the wild, scorpions generally live for two to six years. Some may even live for up to ten years.

The Legendary Scorpion

The scorpion has been feared and respected by people for many centuries. Because of its sting and its secretive nature this animal has often appeared in myths and superstitious legends as an evil creature. It was said to have stung the Greek god Orion to death after he boasted he could kill any animal on Earth. For punishing Orion for being so vain, the scorpion was rewarded by being placed in heaven. There is a constellation (group of stars) in the Milky Way that the Romans named Scorpius—Latin for "scorpion"—and the Greeks even called one of the zodiac signs Scorpio.

Many of the old stories that people told about scorpions are wrong. For example, the stories about these animals committing suicide by stinging themselves to death or crawling into fire are not true.

Words to Know

Abdomen The large rear section of an insect or arachnid.

Antivenin A medicine that can be given to someone who has been stung by a scorpion to stop the poison from working.

Arachnid The group of animals that includes spiders, mites, daddy-longlegs, and scorpions.

Carnivore An animal that eats other animals.

Cephalothorax The front section of an arachnid that is made by the head and thorax being joined together.

Digest To break down food so that an animal's body can get at the important parts it needs to survive.

Exoskeleton The tough outer skin of an insect or scorpion.

Fertilize The joining of a female's eggs and a male's sperm.

Mate To come together to produce young.

Molt Shedding old skin, fur, or feathers to make way for new.

Neurotoxin A poison that stops a victim's nerves from working.

Nocturnal Active at night.

Pectine The sensitive "feelers" underneath a scorpion's body.

Prey An animal that another animal hunts for food.

Spermatophore The packet of sperm from a male scorpion.

Thorax The middle one of the three sections of an insect's body.

INDEX

Cover Photo: Stephen Dalton / NHPA
Photo Credits: Jane Burton / Bruce Coleman, page 4; Jacques Delacour / Still Pictures, page 7; Stephen Dalton / NHPA, pages 8, 12; Daniel Heuclin / NHPA, pages 11, 15, 19, 20, 28, 31, 34, 41, 45; Kim Taylor / Bruce Coleman, page 16; Mazquiaran-UNEP / Still Pictures, page 23; John Shaw / NHPA, page 24; Rod Williams / Bruce Coleman, page 27; Xavier Eichaker / Still Pictures, page 37; Joe McDonald / Bruce Coleman, page 38; Jany Sauvanet / NHPA, page 42.